CW01650896

Pre-19[illegible]sics

Charles Dickens

David Orme

Folens Publishers

Acknowledgements

Folens allows photocopying of pages marked 'copiable page' for educational use, providing that this use is within the confines of the purchasing institution. Copiable pages should not be declared in any return in respect of any photocopying licence.

Folens books are protected by international copyright laws. All rights are reserved. The copyright of all materials in this book, except where otherwise stated, remains the property of the publisher and authors. No part of this publication may be reproduced, stored in a retrieval system, or transmitted, in any form or by any means, for whatever purpose, without the written permission of Folens Limited.

David Orme hereby asserts his moral right to be identified as the author of this work in accordance with the Copyright, Designs and Patents Act 1988.

Editor: Terry Vittachi
Layout artist: Philippa Jarvis
Illustrations: Tony O'Donnell – Graham-Cameron Illustration
Cover image: *Puss in Boots* by Sir John Everett Millais
Cover design: Ed Gallagher and Gary Ward

A Kestrel for a Knave by Barry Hines. Reproduced by permission of Penguin UK.
'A Night at a Cottage' by Richard Hughes. Reproduced by permission of David Higham Associates.
'Glasgow Sonnet' from *Poems of Thirty Years* by Edwin Morgan. Reproduced by permission of Carcanet Press Limited.

© 2000 Folens Limited, on behalf of the author.

Every effort has been made to contact copyright holders of material used in this book. If any have been overlooked, we will be pleased to make any necessary arrangements.

First published 2000 by Folens Limited, Dunstable and Dublin.

Folens Limited, Albert House, Apex Business Centre, Boscombe Road, Dunstable, LU5 4RL, United Kingdom.

ISBN 1 84163 512 X

Contents

Teachers' notes

Great Expectations

While *Great Expectations* is, by Dickens' standards, relatively short, it is nevertheless a substantial read for students. For the inexperienced reader the great number of characters, scenes and events, not all of which are central to the main thrust of the plot, can be confusing. The temptation, therefore, is to work on the basis of reading key chapters linked by a synopsis, with perhaps a filmed version as back-up. This may serve its purpose as far as an examination is concerned, but it is a pity if the students are not at least encouraged to read the whole thing. After all, what is an examination text for contemporary students was an entertaining weekly read – the equivalent of the television soap opera of today – for the Victorian audience.

It is difficult to understand *Great Expectations* fully without reference to the historical events and social concerns of the period. The novel is set at the time of Dickens' own childhood, and the circumstances of his early life inform the novel. Wider reading on the historical background is therefore essential and should form part of the study of *Great Expectations*.

Why do we continue to read Dickens, with his long, ramshackle plots, in the age of the (supposedly) short attention span? One of the chief delights is his humour and his irony. This rarely comes over in film and television versions. Modern students may need sensitising to the language of Dickens, but for some, at least, the effort will be well worth it.

The sheets

It is recommended that the sheets are discussed with the students before they undertake the tasks. Some tasks involve discussions and group work; others are suitable for individual writing exercises.

Background

Pages 6–9 give details of Dickens' own life and information on the main areas of social concern at the time the novel is set. Some pages involve extracts from other Dickens novels. Wider reading beyond this, including further works by Dickens, would be beneficial. Note that, on page 9, students are asked to identify what is unusual about an extract; it is written in one long sentence.

What happens

Pages 10–11 give a short synopsis of the novel, using the original plan of 37 weekly instalments. If teachers wish to establish the level of students' knowledge of the plot, selected sections could be blanked out before copying. Alternatively, the sheets can be left complete for reference.

Key chapters

Pages 12–20 provide further information and activities on the most important chapters in the novel. The tasks are designed to clarify events and issues in each chapter and should be tackled following a careful reading.

Revision

Page 21 asks students to fill in character names in a very simplified synopsis of the novel. Most students should manage this without reference to the text, or the fuller synopsis on pages 10–11. Students who need more assistance could be given this earlier synopsis to help them.

Characters

Pip

Pages 22–24 explore the central character of Pip as a child, a young man, and an adult as he appears at the very end of the novel. The key issues are Pip's development throughout his life, and Dickens' use of the autobiographical device to allow Pip to comment on himself at a younger age.

Other characters

Pages 25–32 give a structure for the student to make notes, including finding key quotations. Some pages include more extended writing and discussion activities to deepen understanding of the characters.

Minor characters

Page 33 has two activities: one involves writing about a minor character, and the other identifying characters from quotations.

Motives

Page 34 lists various actions in the play and asks students to identify the motives of the characters involved. An alternative to free choice is to allocate the various short accounts to students.

Themes

Pages 35–39 cover the key themes of 'Youth and maturity', 'Class distinction and snobbery,' 'Revenge', 'Blighted childhood' and 'Justice and injustice'. Some students may benefit from extended discussion before starting these sheets.

Language

Humour

Page 40 is a very challenging one, but it is

Teachers' notes

important that it should be covered as it attempts to explain the continuing appeal of Dickens today. Further explanation of terms such as 'irony' and 'understatement' might be needed.

Point of view

Page 41 looks at the possibilities inherent in using a first person 'autobiographical' approach. A useful back-up to this page would be to ask students to undertake a piece of writing of their own, with themselves as the central character looking back on an imaginary incident from earlier in their lives.

Extraordinary characters

Page 42 explores how the dialogue, and even the names, of Dickens' characters reveal something about them. The section referring to names from other Dickens novels could be followed up to see how accurate the students' guesses are, although this is intended as an entertaining, optional activity.

Setting

Page 43 asks students to pick out words and phrases used by Dickens to describe various places in the novel. It is worth extending the point made in the first paragraph through discussion.

Structure

Page 44 explores how the original form of the novel – a magazine serialisation – imposes a structure unlike most contemporary novels. In particular, regular 'cliff-hangers' are important to keep the reader interested. A less positive feature is the episodic nature of the plot. Explore through discussion the link that is made between *Great Expectations* and a popular soap opera.

Revision

Page 45 can be set as an individual assignment or be worked through as a class or group discussion.

'The Signalman'

Pages 46–52 offer support to a study of this short story by Charles Dickens. Topics covered are 'Structure,' 'Building atmosphere and tension', 'Characters' and 'Supernatural or psychological?'. This last is the most challenging page and will require support.

A further page is a template for comparing 'The Signalman' with another ghost story. To fulfil exam requirements to compare the text with a more modern one, 'A Night at a Cottage' (pages 58–59) is a possible choice. An interesting alternative would be the banquet scene from *Macbeth*, although this would not, on its own, fulfil the syllabus requirements; however, any other modern ghost story familiar to the students or the teacher would be appropriate.

The section concludes with essay practice and an examination practice sheet.

Wider reading

A Kestrel for a Knave

This section on pages 53–56 fulfils the requirements to study a twentieth-century text alongside *Great Expectations*. *A Kestrel for a Knave* makes a good comparison with *Great Expectations*, both for its similarities and its differences. Both involve a young person whose aspirations lie beyond the poverty of their background. Blighted childhood, class distinction, injustice and revenge are important themes in both, and both books make use of dialect. The major differences are that *A Kestrel for a Knave* is an overtly 'modern' novel, covering a short time span and with a single plot line. Its point of view (third person) is also in contrast with *Great Expectations*. The first three sheets can be worked on without reading *A Kestrel for a Knave* in its entirety, as texts are included. The final page requires a reading of the whole novel.

'Glasgow Sonnet'

This poem by Edwin Morgan on page 57 makes a useful comparison with the 'Barnard's Inn' section of *Great Expectations*. It can also be compared with the extract from *A Kestrel for a Knave* included on page 53.

'A Night at a Cottage'

This short story by Richard Hughes on pages 58–59 makes an interesting comparison with 'The Signalman'. Both stories are written in the first person, although by very different characters. Both stories depend on the depiction of scene to build atmosphere. Both stories rely on a 'twist' at the end, and both scatter clues about the ending throughout the narrative. For students requiring more assistance, discuss the story in detail before asking them to work on the assignment.

Exam practice

Two extracts are provided on pages 60–61, with typical compulsory examination questions for each.

Essay practice

Templates are provided for three practice essays on character, plot and theme: 'The life of Pip', 'Turning points' and 'Revenge'.

Life and times of Charles Dickens

FOCUS

- To gain insight into the themes of *Great Expectations* by learning about Dickens' life.

Introduction
The events in Charles Dickens' own life had a great effect on his writing, and he could never forget the difficulties he and his family had gone through.

1. Read this selection of facts about Charles Dickens' life.

Charles Dickens was born in Portsmouth in 1812. His father, John Dickens, was a clerk in the Navy Pay Office. There were eight children in the family, and they lived variously in Portsmouth, in London and in Chatham.

The family suffered many financial crises, and at the age of 12 Charles was sent to work in a factory, sticking labels on bottles for six shillings a week. Eventually John Dickens was arrested for debt and sent to the debtors' prison, where he was forced to live with his entire family – with the exception of Charles, who visited them in the prison every Sunday.

Later Charles was able to attend school, where he did well. He became a freelance reporter and, eventually, a novelist.

2. *Great Expectations* is sometimes called 'Dickens' most autobiographical novel'. Using the information above, find the parallels between Dickens' life and the themes in *Great Expectations*, and fill in the chart below.

Dickens' own life	Themes and events in *Great Expectations*

3. *Great Expectations* is set, not in the 1860s when it was written, but in the early part of the century. Why do you think Dickens chose to do this?

 © Folens (copiable page)

Child labour in nineteenth-century England

FOCUS

- To gain awareness of the extent of child labour in England in the nineteenth century.

Introduction

At the age of 12 Charles Dickens was sent to work in a London factory, pasting labels on bottles. He used this experience in *David Copperfield*. Read this extract.

Murdstone and Grinby's warehouse was at the waterside. It was a crazy old house with a wharf of its own, abutting on the water when the tide was in, and on the mud when the tide was out, and literally overrun with rats. Its panelled rooms, discoloured with the dirt and smoke of a hundred years, I dare say, its decaying floors and staircase, the squeaking and scuffling of the old grey rats down in the cellars, and the dirt and rottenness of the place, are things not of many years ago, in my mind, but of the present instant.

I know that a great many empty bottles were one of the consequences of their traffic, and that certain men and boys were employed to examine them against the light, and reject those that were flawed, and to rinse and wash them. When the empty bottles ran short, there were labels to be pasted on full ones, or corks to be fitted in them or seals to be put upon the corks, or finished bottles to be packed in casks. All this work was my work, and of the boys employed upon it I was one.

This letter was published in the *Leeds Mercury* in 1830.

... thousands of our fellow-creatures and fellow-subjects, both male and female, the inhabitants of a Yorkshire town ... are at this very moment existing in a state of slavery more horrid than are the victims of that hellish system – colonial slavery ... they are compelled, not by the cart-whip of the slave-driver, but by the dread of the equally appalling thong or strap of the overlooker, to hasten half-dressed to those magazines of British Infantile Slavery – the Worsted Mill of Bradford! Thousands of little children are daily compelled to labour, from six o'clock in the morning to seven in the evening with ... only thirty minutes allowed for eating and recreation ...

- In 1833 the Factory Act was passed. No child under nine was allowed to work; children aged nine to 12 could work up to nine hours a day, and must have at least two hours of schooling.

1. In 1857 Prince Albert (the husband of Queen Victoria) said that, for the working man, children were 'part of his productive power', and that if the children of working families were not allowed to work, it would 'almost paralyse their domestic existence'. Discuss what this tells us about the attitude of adults towards children in the nineteenth century.

2. In Chapter 4 of *Oliver Twist* Dickens describes the fate of a parish apprentice:

   If the master finds, upon a short trial, that he can get enough work out of a boy without putting too much food into him, he shall have him for a term of years, to do what he likes with.

   Read the rest of Chapter 4 of *Oliver Twist* and then write a short comparison between Oliver's experience as an apprentice, and Pip's experience as an apprentice at the hands of Joe in *Great Expectations*.

© Folens (copiable page)

Background

Crime and punishment

FOCUS

- To consider some of the forms of punishment meted out to prisoners in the early nineteenth century.

Introduction

By 1860, when *Great Expectations* was written, some of the forms of punishment it details were already abolished. Prisoners were treated humanely by the standards of the time; many people complained that reforms had gone too far and that prisoners were better fed and housed than people outside, which was an incentive to commit crime so that the 'comforts' of prison could be enjoyed.

1. Prison hulks were ships which were no longer fit for service; they were used as offshore prisons. The last prison hulk ended its days in 1857. Discuss the the advantages of using 'hulks' as prisons.

2. On Pip's arrival in London (Chapter 20) he sees preparations for a public hanging. Public hanging was abolished in 1868, and capital punishment was finally abolished in 1965. Discuss why public hanging was considered a good thing.

3. Pip is shown 'the Debtors' Door, out of which culprits came to be hanged'. Debtors were punished by imprisonment, or even death. In 1824 Dickens' father, John Dickens, was imprisoned for debt. Discuss whether you think imprisonment is an appropriate or effective punishment for people who get into debt.

4. Transportation (shipping offenders to colonies overseas) lasted until the 1840s. Discuss what you think are the good and bad features of transportation from the point of view of:

   a. the authorities

   b. the offenders.

5. Dickens sets his novel at a time before prison reforms. Write down the reasons you think he might have had for doing this. (Think of the plot of the story – the life of Magwitch, for example – as well as Dickens' own background and his concern for social conditions.)

© Folens (copiable page)

Poverty

FOCUS

- To examine the causes of poverty in the early nineteenth century.

Introduction

During the war with France (1793–1809) corn ships were blockaded, so corn prices were high. This made the farmers prosperous, although for the poor it meant expensive bread. After the war, prices fell. Farmers faced more difficult times, so agricultural labourers were paid low wages or lost their jobs.

- After 1815 factories producing war goods such as munitions or uniforms were forced to find new markets; many went out of business.
- Tariff barriers were erected against British goods by continental governments.
- The industrial revolution increasingly meant that skilled craftspeople, such as weavers, found that machines were taking over their work. In the countryside threshing machines were used, and thousands of agricultural workers were laid off.
- Descriptions of poverty frequently appeared in the novels of Charles Dickens, and he was a strong campaigner for better conditions. Read this extract from *The Old Curiosity Shop.*

> Damp, rotten houses, many to let, many yet building, many half-built – and mouldering away – lodgings, where it would be hard to tell which needed pity most, those who let or those who came to take – children, scantily fed and clothed, spread over every street, and sprawling in the dust – scolding mothers, stamping their slipshod feet with noisy threats upon the pavement – shabby fathers, hurrying with dispirited looks to the occupation which brought them 'daily bread' and little more – mangling-women, washerwomen, cobblers, tailors, chandlers, driving their trades in parlours and kitchens and back rooms and garrets, and sometimes all of them under the same roof – brickfields skirting gardens paled with staves of old casks, or timber pillaged from houses burned down, and blackened and blistered by the flames – mounds of dock-weed, nettles, coarse grass, and oyster shells heaped in rank confusion – small dissenting chapels to teach, with no lack of illustration, the miseries of earth, and plenty of new churches, erected with a little superfluous wealth, to show the way to heaven.

1. Discuss whether or not you find anything unusual about the way this extract is written. (Look carefully at the punctuation!) Does this make the description more or less effective?

2. Dickens frequently includes scenes of poverty in his novels. Discuss whether or not you think this is an effective way of campaigning for better conditions.

The plot outline

FOCUS

- To develop an understanding of the plot of *Great Expectations.*

Introduction

The plots of Dickens' novels are complex. For the first readers of *Great Expectations* this was particularly difficult, as the novel appeared as a serial in weekly instalments. This outline will help with your understanding of the plot. Each section represents one instalment of the serial.

Part One

Chapter	Event
1–2	We meet Pip, Magwitch, Joe and Mrs Joe. Pip encounters Magwitch and steals food for him.
3–4	Christmas dinner at the forge. We meet Pumblechook and Wopsle. The soldiers arrive.
5	The search for the convicts on the marshes.
6–7	Life at the forge. Pip is invited to Satis House.
8	Pip's first visit to Satis House. We meet Miss Havisham and Estella.
9–10	Pip decides to improve himself. He receives money from a stranger in the Jolly Bargemen.
11	Pip's second visit to Satis House. He meets the Pockets and Mr Jaggers. Fights with Herbert.
12–13	Further visits to Satis House. Pip is apprenticed to Joe.
14–15	Pip is increasingly dissatisfied with his lot. He revisits Miss Havisham. Joe fights with Orlick. Mrs Joe is attacked.
16–17	The effect of the attack on Mrs Joe. Pip's relationship with Biddy.
18	The visit of Jaggers. Pip is told he has 'great expectations'.
19	Pip prepares to go to London.

© Folens (copiable page)

Part Two

Chapter	Event
20–21	Pip arrives in London. Interview with Jaggers. He meets Wemmick, and meets Herbert again.
22	We learn more about Herbert, and see the Pockets at home.
23–24	Dinner with the Pockets; we meet Drummle and Startop and learn more of Wemmick.
25–26	Dinner at Wemmick's house and at Jaggers'. We meet Molly.
27–28	Joe visits Pip and brings a message from Miss Havisham. He overhears a strange story from a convict on the coach.
29	Pip revisits Satis House. He meets Estella, now an adult.
30–31	Pip returns to London without visiting Joe. Pip and Herbert see Wopsle playing Hamlet.
32–33	Estella comes to London. Pip takes her to Richmond.
34–35	Pip is increasingly in debt. Mrs Joe dies. The funeral.
36–37	Pip's coming of age. He revisits Walworth. Pip secretly funds Herbert's career.
38	Pip sees Estella at Richmond and at Satis House. He is increasingly jealous of the attention Drummle pays to her.
39	Magwitch arrives in London and reveals he is Pip's patron.

Part Three

Chapter	Event
40	Pip finds lodgings for Magwitch and discusses the truth of his expectations with Jaggers.
41–42	Pip and Herbert decide that Magwitch must leave the country. Magwitch tells them his life story.
43–44	Pip meets Drummle in Kent. He confronts Miss Havisham and Estella. Estella reveals she is to marry Drummle.
45–46	Pip learns that Magwitch is being watched. Herbert and Pip move him to Clara's house.
47–48	Pip discovers Compeyson has been watching him. He realises Estella is Molly's daughter.
49–50	Miss Havisham begs Pip's forgiveness, then is badly burned. Back in London, Pip realises that Magwitch is Estella's father.
51–52	Pip confronts Jaggers about Estella. Pip and Herbert plan to get Magwitch abroad. Pip receives a letter from Orlick, without realising who has written it.
53	Orlick attempts to murder Pip, who is rescued by Herbert and Startop.
54	The failed attempt to send Magwitch abroad; he is arrested.
55–56	Magwitch is condemned to death. Herbert goes abroad. Wemmick is married. The death of Magwitch.
57	Pip is ill. When he recovers, he finds that Joe has paid his debts.
58	Pip returns to his home town intending to marry Biddy, but finds she is about to be married to Joe. Pip goes abroad.
59	After 11 years, Pip returns to England and meets Estella again.

© Folens (copiable page)

The novel opens

FOCUS

- To study the opening chapters of *Great Expectations*.

Introduction
The opening chapters give the reader essential background information. This includes introducing key characters and giving information on their backgrounds. They set the scene, get the action under way, and persuade the reader to read on.

1. Make notes detailing what you have learned in the opening chapters.

Characters and their background	The action

2. Write a paragraph explaining how Dickens uses the description of the scene and weather in the graveyard to create atmosphere and reflect the feelings of the characters.

3. Chapters 1 and 2 of *Great Expectations* first appeared in the magazine *All the Year Round* on 1 December 1860. Sales were declining, and it was important to increase the readership. Imagine you are one of those first readers. Discuss the effectiveness of this first instalment in persuading you to buy the next issue. How does Dickens set out to achieve this?

© Folens (copiable page)

Satis House

FOCUS

- A detailed study of Chapter 8.

Introduction
In this chapter Pip first visits Satis House and meets Miss Havisham and Estella. This experience has a major effect on Pip, and changes the course of his life. Even though he is still young, Pip's lifelong love for Estella starts here; it is an example of 'love at first sight'.

1. Read this extract:

"Let me see you play cards with this boy."
"With this boy! Why, he is a common labouring-boy!"
I thought I overheard Miss Havisham's answer – only it seemed so unlikely – "Well? You can break his heart."

Pip does not understand the meaning of Miss Havisham's comment. Nor does the reader at this stage of the novel. Write a sentence explaining:

- what Pip might understand by this remark;
- what it might suggest to the reader.

2. When the whole novel has been read, this comment is more understandable. Complete this sentence:
This remark by Miss Havisham is the first indication that:

____

3. This is the way Chapter 8 ends:

I set off on the four-mile walk to our forge; pondering, as I went along, on all I had seen, and deeply revolving that I was a common labouring-boy; that my hands were coarse, that my boots were thick; that I had fallen into a despicable habit of calling knaves Jacks; that I was much more ignorant than I had considered myself last night, and generally that I was in a low-lived bad way.

Fill in this 'before and after' table, showing the effect of the visit to Satis House on Pip's feelings about himself and his family.

Before	**After**

Great expectations

FOCUS

- A detailed study of Chapters 18–19.

Introduction

Pip is informed by Mr Jaggers that he has 'great expectations'. This is particularly pleasing to Pip, as he has become dissatisfied with his life at the forge. The identity of the benefactor is a secret, although Pip assumes (wrongly) that it is Miss Havisham.

1. Read the conversation between Jaggers and Mr Wopsle in Chapter 18. On a separate sheet, write one sentence describing what this tells us about Jaggers.

2. The importance of Chapter 19 is in what it tells us of the developing character of Pip. The way he treats Joe and Biddy is the key to understanding this. Here are some 'key quotations' from the chapter.

   "It's a pity now, Joe", said I, "that you did not get on a little more, when we had our lessons here; isn't it?"

   What I had meant was, that when I came into my property and was able to do something for Joe, it would have been much more agreeable if he had been better qualified for a rise in station.

   "Joe is a dear good fellow – in fact, I think he is the dearest fellow that ever lived – but he is rather backward in some things. For instance, Biddy, in his learning and his manners."

   Write a sentence saying what you think these quotations tell us about Pip at this point in the story.

3. In Chapter 19, Biddy talks about Joe's pride. Find this passage and read it through. Discuss what Biddy means. In what way does Pip misunderstand her?

4. In Chapter 18 we read this sentence:

   Oh dear good Joe, whom I was so ready to leave and so unthankful to …

   In these words, and the rest of the paragraph, we hear the voice of the adult Pip looking back at, and commenting on, his own behaviour. Read through the two chapters and write out any further quotations that show the adult Pip commenting on himself as a young man.

5. Discuss what hints these quotations give about events later in the book.

© Folens (copiable page)

Joe's visit

FOCUS

- A detailed study of Chapter 27.

- At the start of Chapter 27, Pip receives a letter from Biddy. It tells him that Joe is coming to London and would like to see him. Pip describes his reaction to the news in this way:

> Not with pleasure, though I was bound to him by so many ties; no; with considerable disturbance, some mortification, and a keen sense of incongruity. If I could have kept him away by paying money, I certainly would have paid money. My greatest reassurance was, that he was coming to Barnard's Inn, not to Hammersmith, and consequently would not fall in Bentley Drummle's way. I had little objection to him being seen by Herbert or his father, for both of whom I had a respect; but I had the sharpest sensitiveness as to him being seen by Drummle, whom I held in contempt. So, throughout life, our worst weaknesses and meannesses are usually committed for the sake of the people whom we most despise.

1. Make sure you fully understand the meaning of *mortification* and *incongruity*. Then discuss Pip's attitude to Joe.
2. After your discussion, sum up Pip's attitude in one sentence.
3. Write the last sentence of the above extract in your own words, making its meaning clear.
4. At the end of the chapter, Joe describes his own feelings. Read this paragraph now, and write down any key quotations that sum up Joe's attitude.
5. Discuss what the comic writing about Joe's hat tells us about the feelings of the characters. Why does Dickens include this?

Pip meets Estella again

FOCUS

- A detailed study of Chapter 29.

Introduction

In this chapter Pip returns to Satis House and meets Estella once more. This is an important chapter in gaining understanding of Pip's love for Estella, and of the character of Estella herself.

1. At the beginning of the chapter Pip has not seen Estella since they were children, yet he still loves her and believes it is Miss Havisham's intention that they should be married. In the second paragraph he describes the nature of his love for her. Read these quotations and discuss their meaning.

   I did not … invest her with any attributes save those she possessed.

   I loved her simply because I found her irresistible.

2. Pip is speaking as an adult looking back at his youth. This is made clear in comments such as:

   I slipped hopelessly back into the coarse and common boy again.

   She treated me as a boy still, but she lured me on.

   At the time of writing, then, the adult Pip would be aware that all is not as it seems; Miss Havisham's intentions and Estella's background and nature, for example. In the light of your knowledge of the rest of the story, complete these sentences:

   Pip thinks that Miss Havisham ______________________________

   However, we learn later that ______________________________

   Pip thinks that Estella comes from ______________________________

   However, we learn later that she is ______________________________

3. Write down your answers to the following questions.

   – Why does Dickens not tell us these facts now?

   Estella tells Pip that she has "no heart – if that has anything to do with my memory".

   – What does this mean?

   – What has made her 'heartless'?

   – Do you think this statement is true?

© Folens (copiable page)

The arrival of Magwitch

FOCUS

- A detailed study of Chapter 39.

- In this chapter Magwitch returns illegally from Australia to tell Pip that he is his benefactor.

1. Dickens does not allow Magwitch to reveal that he is the benefactor straight away. Discuss the effect of this slow revelation on Pip, and upon the reader.
2. Consider Pip's immediate reaction, and then his realisation of the longer term implications of the news. Then fill in this chart.

Pip's immediate feelings on hearing the news are …	Once Pip has had time to absorb all the implications of the news, he realises that…

3. Dickens makes use of powerful imagery and creation of atmosphere to underline that this is a crucial moment in the novel. Discuss his reasons for using images of storm, shipwreck and death in this chapter.
4. Use the ideas raised in your discussion to write a paragraph showing why Dickens' use of imagery is so effective in Chapter 39.

© Folens (copiable page)

Confrontation at Satis House

FOCUS

- A detailed study of Chapter 44.

Introduction
This is an important chapter in understanding the increasing maturity of Pip. He revisits Satis House and confronts Miss Havisham with the way she has used him. Discuss the following questions.

1. What does Pip accuse Miss Havisham of?

2. What arguments does Pip use in his attempt to persuade Estella that he loves her and that she should not marry Drummle?

3. Read these remarks of Estella's:

   "When you say you love me, I know what you mean, as a form of words; but nothing more. You address nothing in my breast, you touch nothing there … I have tried to warn you of this; now, have I not?"

   "It is in *my* nature … It is in the nature formed within me."

   "Should I fling myself away upon the man who would the soonest feel … that I took nothing to him?"

   "Don't be afraid of my being a blessing to him."

   What does Estella mean by these remarks? Why does she say that she cannot marry Pip?

4. Write down any further remarks by Estella that help the reader to understand her attitude.

5. Discuss and compare the behaviour of Pip during his visit to Satis House in Chapter 44 with his behaviour during his visit in Chapter 29. How is it different?

 © Folens (copiable page)

The death of Miss Havisham

FOCUS

- A detailed study of Chapter 49.

Introduction
In this chapter we see the final encounter of Pip and Miss Havisham, and we discover that both characters have changed. The chapter ends with the dramatic burning of Miss Havisham.

1. Write a paragraph on Miss Havisham as she appears in this chapter. It has been started for you. Make sure that you include quotations from the chapter.

In Chapter 49 Miss Havisham finally realises …

2. Miss Havisham's final wish is that Pip should forgive her. Write out one key quotation that shows that Pip is able to do so.

3. Discuss what this tells us about Pip at this stage of the novel.

© Folens (copiable page)

The ending

FOCUS

- To examine the two endings of *Great Expectations*.

Introduction

Once Dickens had finished the final chapters, he gave them to a friend to look at. The friend did not like the ending, and suggested a different one. Dickens agreed.

Here is the original ending. It starts with Pip talking to Biddy in the final chapter.

"Tell me as an old, old friend. Have you quite forgotten her?"

"My dear Biddy, I have forgotten nothing in my life that ever had a foremost place there. But that poor dream, as I once used to call it, has all gone by. Biddy, all gone by."

It was two years more, before I saw herself. I had heard of her as leading a most unhappy life, and as being separated from her husband who had used her with great cruelty, and who had become quite renowned as a compound of pride, brutality and meanness. I had heard of the death of her husband (from an accident consequent on ill-treating a horse), and of her being married again to a Shropshire doctor, who, against his interest, had once very manfully interposed, on an occasion when he was in professional attendance on Mr Drummle, and had witnessed some outrageous treatment of her. I had heard that the Shropshire doctor was not rich, and that they lived on her own personal fortune.

I was in England again – in London, and walking along Piccadilly with little Pip – when a servant came running after me to ask would I step back to a lady in a carriage who wished to speak to me. It was a little pony carriage, which the lady was driving; and the lady and I looked sadly enough on one another.

"I am greatly changed, I know; but I thought you would like to shake hands with Estella too, Pip. Lift up that pretty child and let me kiss it!" (She supposed the child, I think, to be my child.)

I was very glad afterwards to have had the interview, for, in her face and in her voice, and in her touch, she gave me the assurance, that suffering had been stronger than Miss Havisham's teaching, and had given her a heart to understand what my heart used to be.

1. Now that you have read this, reconsider the published book. Some readers say it has a 'happy' ending, but others say that it is ambiguous (does not have a clear meaning). Re-read the final words:

   I saw the shadow of no
   parting from her.

   Discuss what you think this means.

2. Now list the key differences between the final published version and the original one, above. Which makes the better ending, and why? Which ending do you prefer?

 © Folens (copiable page)

The plot

FOCUS

- To revise the key events in the plot.

1. These are the key events in the novel. The names of some of the characters are missing. Write the correct order in the box, and fill in the names. The first box has been numbered for you.

___________ meets the convict ______________ in a graveyard. [1]	_________ and ____________ attempt to get ____________ out of the country, but he is arrested. [ ]	_____________ tells Pip that she is going to marry ________________ . [ ]
_____________ tries to kill ____________ at the limekilns. [ ]	_____________ dies in prison. [ ]	In London, ____________ becomes friends with ___________ but finds he is ashamed of his family, especially _________ [ ]
___________ goes to play at Satis House. He meets ______________ and ________________ . [ ]	___________ tells Pip that ___________ has died. [ ]	The lawyer ____________ tells ___________ that he has 'great expectations'. [ ]
___________ is ill. When he recovers, he finds that ___________ has paid off his debts. [ ]	___________ falls increasingly into debt. [ ]	______________ returns from Australia and reveals himself as _______'s benefactor. [ ]
___________ returns to Satis House and meets ___________ again. [ ]	______________________ is burned in a fire after begging _______ to forgive her. [ ]	___________ goes to live in London. [ ]

2. The final chapters have not been included in this summary. Summarise the final events of *Great Expectations*.

Young Pip

FOCUS

- To examine the character of Pip as a boy in Chapters 1–17.

1. Which of the qualities listed here could apply to Pip as a boy? If you agree with them, find evidence to support them. If you do not agree, say why. Use the empty boxes for ideas of your own.

Quality	We see this when …
kind-hearted	
gullible	
conscious of his inferior position	
obedient	
imaginative	
loyal	

2. In once sentence, sum up other characters' views of Pip.

   Joe sees Pip as ____________________

   Mrs Joe sees Pip as ____________________

   Estella sees Pip as ____________________

3. Now choose another character from these early chapters and give their view of Pip.

   ____________ sees Pip as ____________________

4. 'As a child, Pip is told what to do; he is never allowed to decide things for himself and he never does so.' Discuss whether or not you agree with this statement.

© Folens (copiable page)

Pip as a young man

FOCUS

- To examine the character of Pip as a young man in Chapters 18–57.

Introduction

The major part of *Great Expectations* shows Pip as a young man. During this part of the book he moves to London, learns gentlemanly behaviour, begins to slide into debt, rejects his humble background, meets Estella again, learns who his benefactor is, and eventually loses his money.

1. When you looked at the character of the young Pip, you considered these weaknesses and qualities in his character:

   - kindness
   - consciousness of his inferior background
   - imagination
   - gullibility
   - obedience
   - loyalty

   Discuss which of these characteristics you think Pip still possesses as a young man.

2. Here are some more characteristics. Do you agree that they apply to Pip as a young man? If so, find evidence for them. Use the empty boxes to write down ideas of your own.

Quality	We see this when …
arrogance	
ingratitude	
foolishness	
steadfastness	

3. Use the information you have gathered on this page, together with your ideas on Pip as a boy, to write a paragraph describing how Pip's character changes when he moves to London. Use these openings:

   – Before Pip came to London he was …

   – However, once he was there …

Pip as an adult

FOCUS

- To examine the character of the adult Pip at the end of the book, and his role as narrator and commentator.

Introduction
We meet the adult Pip only very briefly, in the final chapter, when he returns from abroad. However, we can learn more about him from his increasing maturity before and after the death of Magwitch (Chapters 56–58), and his role as narrator throughout the book.

1. On a separate sheet, list the key events in Chapters 56–58 that demonstrate Pip's increasing maturity.

2. Discuss the way Pip's relationship with Joe changes towards the end of the book.

Throughout the book, Pip steps outside the action of the story and comments directly upon it. An example is at the end of Chapter 9 when Pip writes 'That was a memorable day to me …' Often, these comments describe his faults as a young man: his arrogance, his rejection of Joe, his infatuation and his foolish lifestyle.

3. Find two of these direct comments and write a short paragraph on each, making it clear what they tell us about the character of Pip.

Paragraph 1:

Paragraph 2:

4. Imagine that you are writing your own autobiography (life story). Write a sentence commenting on something that you did when you were younger that, now you are older, you regret or wish you had done differently.

© Folens (copiable page)

Joe Gargery

FOCUS

- To study the character of Joe Gargery.

- Use this page to make notes on the character of Joe.

Your impressions of Joe

At the opening of the novel:

On his visit to London in Chapter 27:

At the end of the novel:

Key quotations that describe him spoken by

Pip:

Biddy:

The actions that demonstrate his character:

towards Mrs Joe ______________________________

towards Pip ______________________________

Consider this statement: 'Joe Gargery represents the moral heart of *Great Expectations*, symbolising goodness, kindness and generosity.'

1. Discuss the way Dickens uses the character of Joe to represent these qualities. (Think about the way he uses Joe and his background to contrast with other characters, places and incidents in the book.)
2. Discuss the way Dickens uses the character of Joe to emphasise the evils of class distinction in the society of the time.

Miss Havisham

FOCUS

- To study the character of Miss Havisham.

- Use this page to make notes on the character of Miss Havisham.

Your impressions of Miss Havisham

In Chapter 8 when Pip first meets her:

In Chapter 44: has she changed? Do we learn anything new about her?

In Chapter 49: has she changed? Do we learn anything new about her?

Key quotations that describe her spoken by

Pip:

Estella:

- **Motivations:** discuss, then make notes on, why Miss Havisham:
  - lives such a bleak, reclusive life
  - brings up Estella in the way she does
  - encourages Pip's love for Estella.

 © Folens (copiable page)

Estella

FOCUS

- To study the character of Estella.

- Use this page to make notes on the character of Estella.

Your impressions of Estella

As a child (Chapters 8 and 11–13):

As an adult:

Key quotations that describe her spoken by

Miss Havisham:

Pip:

Estella herself:

- **Motivations:** discuss, then make notes on, why Estella
  - treats the young Pip with such disdain
  - does not return Pip's love
  - marries Drummle
  - has changed at the very end of the book.

Magwitch

FOCUS

- To study the character of Magwitch.

- Pip's feelings about Magwitch, and the way he describes him, change through the book. Use this page to make notes on Pip's impressions alongside your own.

Your impressions of Magwitch	Pip's impressions of Magwitch
In Chapter 1:	**In Chapter 1:**
In Chapter 39:	**In Chapter 40:**
After hearing his life story (Chapter 42):	**While Magwitch is dying (Chapters 54 and 56):**

- **Motivations:** Discuss, then make notes on, why Magwitch decides to make Pip a gentleman.

© Folens (copiable page)

Mr Jaggers

FOCUS

- To study the character of Mr Jaggers.

- Complete the Jaggers Quiz, then complete the rest of the activities.

Jaggers Quiz

a. When do we first meet Jaggers?

____

b. What does Jaggers tell young Pip that he has? ______________________________

c. In which street is Jaggers' office? ______________________________

d. What is the name of Jaggers' clerk? ______________________________

e. What is the name of Jaggers' servant? ______________________________

f. Name two of Jaggers' clients. ______________________________

g. Find three things that Jaggers says that are typical of his character. ______________________________

____

1. Jaggers keeps secrets; for example, he does not tell Pip that he is wrong in assuming that Miss Havisham is his benefactor. Discuss whether this reflects well or badly on Jaggers.
2. Jaggers is presented as a cold, calculating, heartless lawyer. Discuss whether you think this is fair.
3. Jaggers is often shown washing his hands, like Pontius Pilate in the Bible. Discuss what the washing of hands symbolises. Why do you think Dickens uses this idea?
4. The second time we meet Mr Jaggers is in the Jolly Bargemen, where he has an argument with Mr Wopsle. Write a character sketch based only on the impression he makes in this chapter.

© Folens (copiable page)

Herbert Pocket

FOCUS

- To study the character of Herbert Pocket.

Introduction
Like Pip and Estella, Herbert Pocket is a character we meet as a child and as a young adult. He becomes a good friend to Pip.

1. Discuss which of the words in the table below describe Herbert, which describe Pip, and why. There is space to add more words of your own.

	Herbert	Pip	Why?
easy-going			
snobbish			
extravagant			
well-bred			
generous			
selfish			

2. Clara Barley thinks that Pip is a very bad influence on Herbert. Discuss whether or not you think she is right.

3. We first meet Herbert at Satis House in Chapter 11, where he fights with Pip. Discuss what we learn about Herbert's character. What aspects of Herbert as a child remind us of Herbert as an adult?

4. Chapter 22 describes Pip and Herbert's first meal together. Write a paragraph detailing what this comic episode tells us about the character of Herbert.

5. Write down three of Herbert's actions that illustrate his character.

 © Folens (copiable page)

Drummle and Orlick

FOCUS

- To study the characters and functions of the villains Drummle and Orlick.

- Use this page to discuss and record your ideas on Drummle and Orlick.

Drummle

1. At the beginning of Chapter 25 there is a description of Bentley Drummle. Make a list of the key words in the first paragraph that describe his character and appearance.

2. In Chapter 26 Jaggers describes Drummle as "The blotchy, sprawly, sulky fellow". He goes on to call him "the spider", and warns Pip to "keep as clear of him as you can". Strangely, however, he also says that he likes the look of him. Discuss and answer the following.

   – Why might Jaggers like Drummle?

   – Why does Jaggers choose the name 'spider' for Drummle? (Jaggers has more to say about Drummle in Chapter 48.)

   – Why is Bentley Drummle an important character in *Great Expectations*?

Orlick

3. Orlick appears right through the novel – sometimes when he is least expected. Write a short summary of Orlick's actions in:

   – Chapters 15 and 16

   – Chapter 29

   – Chapter 40

   – Chapter 53.

4. Discuss and answer the following.

   – Why does Orlick have such a hatred of Pip? (Read carefully what Orlick says in Chapter 53.)

   – After Orlick attacks him, Pip is left with a strong feeling of guilt. Why do you think this is?

© Folens (copiable page)

Biddy and Wemmick

FOCUS

- To study the characters and functions of Wemmick and Biddy.

- Use this page to make notes on the characters of Wemmick and Biddy.

1. Pip says that it seems that there are 'twin Wemmicks', one in London and one in Walworth. Write a brief comparison of the two Wemmicks.

Wemmick in London	Wemmick in Walworth

2. Like Joe, Biddy is a model of honesty, humility and morality, and this contrasts strongly with the character of Pip as a young man. Unlike Joe, however, Biddy is prepared to tell Pip about his faults, particularly in Chapter 19. In Chapter 35, through her use of the title 'Mr' and her silences, she makes her feelings very clear to the reader, although in both cases Pip fails to understand her.

   List the main faults Biddy finds in Pip in these two chapters.

3. Discuss what you think is the main function of Biddy as a character in the novel.

 © Folens (copiable page)

Minor characters

FOCUS

- To revise the minor characters in *Great Expectations*.

- Below is a list of some of the minor characters in *Great Expectations*.

1. Choose one and write a brief account of their character and their role in the plot of the novel.

Mrs Joe	**Molly**	**Matthew Pocket**	**Compeyson**
Wopsle	**Startop**	**Uncle Pumblechook**	**Mrs Pocket**

Character:

Their role in the novel:

2. **Quotation Quiz.** Who says what?

"Who brought you up by hand?"

"Play, play, play!"

"I am disgusted with my calling and with my life."

"Get hold of portable property."

"I've made a gentleman on you! It's me what has done it!"

"I am looking about me."

"You must know I have no heart."

"What larks!"

"Of course, you'll go wrong somehow, but that's no fault of mine."

"Oh, you enemy, you enemy!"

Mrs Joe

Motives

FOCUS

- To examine the motives of some of the characters in *Great Expectations*.

- Here are the actions of some of the characters in the novel. Discuss these actions, then choose three of them. In the space provided, write a short account (in the first person) of the possible reasons for their behaviour from the point of view of the character.

1. Miss Havisham invites Pip to Satis House.
2. Jaggers does not tell Pip that Miss Havisham is not his benefactor.

Character	
Action	
Motive	

3. Miss Havisham lets Pip believe that she is his benefactor.
4. Orlick tries to kill Pip.

Character	
Action	
Motive	

5. Pip is ashamed of Joe.
6. Pip secretly gives money to help Herbert.

Character	
Action	
Motive	

© Folens (copiable page)

Youth and maturity

FOCUS

- To examine the theme of character development in *Great Expectations*.

Introduction
Some characters in *Great Expectations* remain the same throughout the book – Joe and Herbert, for example – while others change. In particular, the character of Pip at the end of the book is very different from the Pip who first goes to London. The theme of gaining wisdom and maturity is an important one in *Great Expectations*.

1. These words describe the young Pip. Write down their opposites.

arrogant	**snobbish**	**selfish**	**imprudent**
______________	______________	______________	______________

2. For each of the words you have written, give an example below of how Pip demonstrates this characteristic in his later life.

3. Pip learns a great deal through the example of others. Discuss which characters in particular help him to become more mature, and what it is they demonstrate to him.

4. Pip also learns from some of the more negative characters in the book. Discuss which characters these are, and what he learns from them.

5. Estella is a character who has changed by the end of the novel, although we do not see the mature Estella until the very last page. Here she describes what has changed her:

> "… suffering has been stronger than all other teaching, and has taught me to understand what your heart used to be. I have been bent and broken, but – I hope – into a better shape."

Write a paragraph explaining what Estella means in your own words.

© Folens (copiable page)

Class distinction and snobbery

FOCUS

- To examine the way in which class distinction and snobbery are depicted in *Great Expectations*.

Introduction
Dickens powerfully satirises class distinction and snobbery in the novel.

Miss Havisham – uses wealth and social position in a vindictive attempt to punish others for her own tragedy.

Bentley Drummle – is thoroughly unpleasant, but his wealth and position enable him to get what he wants, including Estella, whom he views as a possession.

Mrs Pocket – is so obsessed with her social position that she neglects her family.

Pip – is keen to join this society, yet his aspirations are built on a lie.

1. On a separate sheet, complete the next two paragraphs in your own words:

   - When Pip first sees Estella, she is above his social class. Pip feels ashamed of his common appearance and manners and wants to improve himself to make himself worthy of her, even though she is superior and snobbish. Yet at the end of the novel we discover that Estella …

   - When Pip learns that he has 'great expectations', he sees this as a way to move out of his lowly social class; but when he discovers the identity of his benefactor, he …

2. Now write a paragraph describing how the confidence trickster Compeyson uses his class background to avoid a heavy punishment. (See Chapter 22.)

3. Choose one of these topics for a short essay:

   a. Write an appreciation of Dickens' description of Mrs Pocket in Chapter 23.

   b. Comment on the behaviour of Pumblechook towards Pip before and after it is learned that he has 'great expectations'.

© Folens (copiable page)

Revenge

FOCUS

- To examine the theme of revenge in *Great Expectations*.

Introduction
Revenge is a key theme of the novel.

1. Complete the following sentences in the space provided.

Miss Havisham seeks revenge on all men because ...	Magwitch seeks revenge on Compeyson because ...
Orlick seeks revenge, first on Mrs Joe, then on Pip, because ...	**The law seeks revenge rather than justice. Examples of this are ...**

2. Discuss the behaviour of these characters compared with that of Joe in the early days at the forge, when Mrs Joe is still alive.

Blighted childhood

FOCUS

- To examine the theme of childhood in *Great Expectations*.

Introduction
In his work Dickens shows his concern for the blighted lives of children. Many of his novels are concerned with children brought up under very difficult circumstances.

1. Look again at the early chapters of *Great Expectations*. Discuss the possible reasons for Mrs Joe's treatment of Pip. Here are some ideas to help you:

   – her own nature **– resentment** **– her life at the forge** **– disappointment**

2. Now discuss the way Miss Havisham brings up Estella. Why does she treat her in this way? What is the result? Can you draw any comparisons between Miss Havisham and Mrs Joe?

3. The upbringing of Drummle and Startop is briefly described in Chapter 25, that of the younger Pocket children in Chapter 23, and that of Magwitch in Chapter 42. Bearing in mind Dickens' theme of blighted childhood, discuss what, if anything, you find surprising about the character of Herbert.

4. In Chapter 42 Magwitch describes his childhood, and the attitude of adults towards him:

   " 'This is a terrible hardened one', they says to prison wisitors, picking out me. 'May be said to live in jails, this boy.' Then they looked at me, and I looked at them, and they measured my head, some on 'em – they had better a measured my stomach – and others on 'em giv me tracts what I couldn't read, and made me speeches what I couldn't understand. They always went on agen me about the Devil. But what the Devil was I to do?"

   Write a paragraph describing the attitude of 'authority' to children such as Abel Magwitch.

5. Read again the Christmas dinner scene in Chapter 4. Write a paragraph describing the views of Mrs Joe, Pumblechook and Wopsle on children.

Wider reading
Look at the opening chapters of *Oliver Twist* and the scenes at Dotheboys Hall in *Nicholas Nickleby*. What view of childhood do these give us?

 © Folens (copiable page)

Justice and injustice

FOCUS

- To examine the theme of justice and injustice in *Great Expectations*.

Introduction

Official justice, as typified by Jaggers, is seen as hopelessly corrupt, and only available to those with the means to pay for it, or who come from the right background. Yet justice is served on the characters in the novel, either by fate or by other characters.

- Discuss this, then fill in the chart below. Tick the box to show whether you think the characters deserve their fate, then write down why you think this.

1. **Joe gains happiness with Biddy.** ☐ deserved ☐ undeserved Why?	2. **Herbert gains happiness with Clara.** ☐ deserved ☐ undeserved Why?
3. **Magwitch dies in prison.** ☐ deserved ☐ undeserved Why?	4. **Pip stays with Estella at the end.** ☐ deserved ☐ undeserved Why?
5. **Estella has an unhappy marriage to Bentley Drummle.** ☐ deserved ☐ undeserved Why?	6. **Miss Havisham dies in a fire.** ☐ deserved ☐ undeserved Why?
	7. **Compeyson dies at the hand of Magwitch.** ☐ deserved ☐ undeserved Why?

Humour

FOCUS

- To examine Dickens' use of humorous language.

Introduction
Dickens' use of humour in his description of events that are often tragic or cruel makes the novels very readable. In some ways the contrast between the humorous language and the serious events makes the account of tragedy and cruelty even more effective.

1. These are some of the techniques Dickens used:

   irony – stating the opposite of the truth

   understatement – describing serious events in a light-hearted or trivial way

   overstatement – describing trivial things or events in a serious way, or using ridiculously grand or pompous language.

   Read the following extracts from Chapter 2 and look for and discuss examples of these techniques. (Remember that what is being described is in fact child abuse, which is far from humorous.)

> At this dismal intelligence, I twisted the only button on my waistcoat round and round, and looked in great depression at the fire. Tickler was a wax-ended piece of cane, worn smooth by collision with my tickled frame.

> My sister, Mrs Joe, throwing the door wide open, and finding an obstruction behind it, immediately divined the cause, and applied Tickler to its further investigation. She concluded by throwing me – I often served her as a connubial missile – at Joe …

> Some medical beast had revived Tar-water in those days as a fine medicine, and Mrs Joe always kept a supply of it in the cupboard; having a belief in its virtues correspondent to its nastiness. At the best of times, so much of this elixir was administered to me as a choice restorative, that I was conscious of going about, smelling like a new fence. On this particular evening the urgency of my case demanded a pint of this mixture, which was poured down my throat, for my greater comfort …

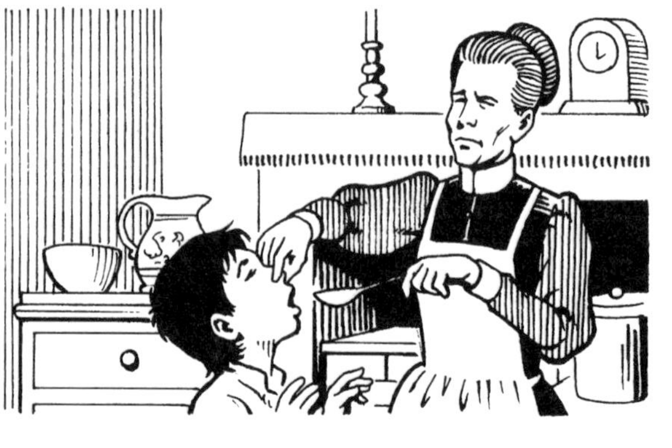

2. Choose a further chapter from *Great Expectations* and write down an example of irony, understatement and overstatement. Suggested chapters are 23 (Pip at the Pockets' house) and 31 (Herbert and Pip at the theatre).

© Folens (copiable page)

Point of view

FOCUS

- To examine Dickens' use of the autobiographical literary technique.

Introduction

Great Expectations is written like an autobiography; that is, we are to suppose that Pip is writing his own life story some time after the events described. Of course, in a real autobiography, it is unlikely that the writer would remember incidents in such detail.

Dickens frequently used this literary technique. It enabled him to write in a very flexible way. Some of the advantages are:

- The central character is able to comment on the action; in particular, Pip comments critically upon himself as a young man which sets the tone of guilt and regret.
- The use of the first person makes the story a very personal one; the reader feels that he or she is 'inside' the mind of the central character.
- We see the younger Pip through the eyes of the adult. Events that are serious to a child are less so to an adult, who can put the events into a wider perspective. In this way the reader gains two perspectives on events, seeing characters such as Pumblechook through the eyes of the child and of the adult Pip.

1. In groups of three, divide the roles of Magwitch, Pip as a child, and Pip as the adult narrator, and then read aloud part of Pip's encounter with Magwitch in the graveyard in Chapter 1.

2. On a separate sheet, write out the extract you have chosen in the third person, using 'he' or 'Pip' instead of 'I'.

© Folens (copiable page)

Extraordinary characters

FOCUS

- To explore Dickens' revelation of character through the use of dialogue.

Introduction
The novels of Dickens are full of extraordinary and eccentric individuals. Apart from direct description, Dickens uses dialogue to reveal their characters.

1. Write out a line of dialogue typical of these characters which reveals something about them.

Jaggers

Joe

Magwitch

2. Choose a different character and write out a line of their dialogue.

3. Dickens was particularly inventive with the names he chose for the people in his novels. Often the names suggest something of the person's character. Look at these names of figures from other Dickens novels. Discuss what kind of personalities their names suggest.

Mr Gradgrind	**Uriah Heep**	**Ebeneezer Scrooge**	**Wackford Squeers**	**Mr Pecksniff**
Mr Bumble	**Lady Dedlock**	**Captain Cuttle**	**Betsy Prig**	**Mrs Miff**

4. Discuss which characters in *Great Expectations* have names that reflect their personalities.

5. Many characters have 'catchphrases' or unusual habits that mark them out. Write out a catchphrase or habit associated with each of these characters.

Mrs Joe ______________________ Herbert ______________________

Joe ______________________ Wemmick ______________________

  © Folens (copiable page)

Setting

FOCUS

- To examine Dickens' use of language depicting setting.

Introduction
Much of the atmosphere in *Great Expectations* is built up by the description of the setting. These descriptions help the reader to understand the feelings and emotions of the characters.

- Here are some settings in *Great Expectations* with particularly powerful descriptions. For each one, select from the text key words that are used to describe it, and one key sentence or phrase, and fill in the boxes.

Setting	Key words	Key sentence
the marshes		
Satis House (exterior)		
Satis House (interior)		
Jaggers' office		
Barnard's Inn		
Newgate Prison		

Serialisation

FOCUS

- To examine the structure of *Great Expectations*.

Introduction

Most of Dickens' novels were published as serials, and the result can be similar to one of today's 'soap operas'. Dickens' first novel, *The Pickwick Papers*, was a series of disconnected events linked by a common set of characters.

There were two important implications for writing a novel in this way. One was that the novels tended to be long, and to contain material not central to the plot – the more issues that could be sold, the better it was for sales. Once someone was 'hooked' on the story, they needed to buy every episode! The other was the importance of regular 'cliffhangers' to keep readers interested and to encourage them to buy the next issue.

This table shows the chapters contained in each issue of *All the Year Round* (the magazine in which *Great Expectations* was first serialised) in 1860 and 1861. Note that the key chapters, with important plot developments, are often double length.

Part One	Part Two	Part Three
1–2	20–21	40
3–4	22	41–42
5	23–24	43–44
6–7	25–26	45–46
8	27–28	47–48
9–10	29	49–50
11	30–31	51–52
12–13	32–33	53
14–15	34–35	54
16–17	36–37	55–56
18	38	57
19	39	58
		59

1. Choose a selection of 'episode endings', looking for dramatic incidents or 'teasers' (hints about future events) that act as cliffhangers, and discuss why they would encourage someone to read more. (You might start with Chapters 4, 15, 17, 21, 38, 42, 44 and 50.)

2. Choose one of the endings you have discussed and write a paragraph describing how Dickens leaves the reader wanting to know more, and how effective you think he is. Remember that contemporary readers would not have known the outline of the story the way you do!

© Folens (copiable page)

Dickens' language

FOCUS

- To examine in detail the use of language in a passage from *Great Expectations*.

- Read this extract from Chapter 19 and write full answers to the questions which follow it. Here, Mr Pumblechook has discovered that Pip has the prospect of a large fortune.

I mentioned to Mr Pumblechook that I wished to have my new clothes sent to his house, and he was ecstatic on my so distinguishing him. I mentioned my reason for desiring to avoid observation in the village, and he lauded it to the skies. There was nobody but himself, he intimated, worthy of my confidence, and – in short, might he? Then he asked me tenderly if I remembered our boyish games at sums, and how we had gone together to have me bound apprentice, and, in effect, how he had ever been my favourite fancy and my chosen friend? If I had taken ten times as many glasses of wine as I had, I should have known that he never had stood in that relation towards me, and should in my heart of hearts have repudiated the idea. Yet for all that, I remember feeling convinced that I had been much mistaken in him, and that he was a sensible practical good-hearted prime fellow.

By degrees he fell to reposing such great confidence in me, as to ask my advice in reference to his own affairs. He mentioned that there was an opportunity for a great amalgamation and monopoly of the corn and seed trade on these premises, if enlarged, such as had never occurred before in that, or any other neighbourhood. What alone was wanting to the realisation of a vast fortune, he considered to be More Capital. Those were the two little words, more capital. Now it appeared to him (Pumblechook) that if that capital were got into the business, through a sleeping partner, sir – which sleeping partner would have nothing to do but walk in, by self or deputy, whenever he pleased, and examine the books – and walk in twice a year and take his profits away in his pocket, to the tune of fifty per cent – it appeared to him that that might be an opening for a young gentleman of spirit combined with property, which would be worthy of his attention. But what did I think? He had great confidence in my opinion, and what did I think? I gave it as my opinion. "Wait a bit!" The united vastness and directness of this view so struck him, that he no longer asked if he might shake hands with me, but said he really must – and did.

1. What impression of himself is Pumblechook trying to present to Pip in this passage?
2. What are Pumblechook's real motives for behaving in this way?
3. Make a list of words that you think describe Pumblechook's behaviour.
4. Find examples of exaggerated, pompous language used by Dickens in the extract. How does he use them to make Pumblechook seem even more ridiculous?
5. How does Dickens, in the voice of the narrator Pip, make the reader aware of what is going on, even if Pip does not grasp fully what is going on at the time?
6. Find an example of Pip reflecting as an adult on this incident. What does this contribute to the passage?
7. This passage describes a hypocritical and self-seeking man getting a young person drunk in the hope of cheating him out of his money. Why does Dickens present this as a comic scene?

© Folens (copiable page)

Structure

FOCUS

- To study the structure of 'The Signalman'.

Introduction
The story of 'The Signalman' is structured around the number three. The narrator visits the signal box three times; and there are three accidents or deaths on the railway.

1. In the space below, give short accounts of what happens.

The narrator's visits
1.
2.
3.

The accidents
1.
2.
3.

2. Dickens gives a sense of structure to the story by making the opening mirror the ending, but with a surprise 'twist'. On a separate sheet, write a paragraph on how he achieves this.

 © Folens (copiable page)

Building atmosphere and tension

FOCUS

- To examine the creation of atmosphere in 'The Signalman'.

Introduction
Ghost stories need a chilling atmosphere to work well. Dickens establishes this atmosphere right at the beginning of the story with his description of the narrator's descent into the cutting.

1. Write out any words and phrases Dickens uses to suggest death and the supernatural in this opening description.

2. Read carefully the signalman's descriptions of the strange apparition by the signal. Discuss whether you think these descriptions are particularly effective in adding to the supernatural feel of the story and, if so, why.

3. Dickens builds tension by building the reader's expectations. Strange events occur, but are not immediately explained. During the narrator's first visit, a number of 'mysteries' are left unsolved. Extend this list with as many more as you can.

- The signalman's alarm at the actions of the narrator
- The signalman's anxiety about the bell

4. Discuss whereabouts in the story Dickens refers directly to the possibility of supernatural events being involved. Why does he mention the possibility at this point?

Characters

FOCUS

- To study the characters in 'The Signalman'.

Introduction
There are only two main characters in the story: the narrator and the signalman.

The narrator

1. The story reveals little about the narrator's background and character. Make notes on what we learn about his background. (Think about the way he speaks to the signalman and what he tells us directly.)

2. Make notes on what we learn about his character. (Think about the possible explanations he offers the signalman for the things that happen.)

The signalman

3. Write a short account of the signalman. Include what we learn from background details and from what the narrator and the railwaymen at the end of the story tell us.

 © Folens (copiable page)

Supernatural or psychological?

FOCUS

- To examine the tension between rational and supernatural elements in ghost stories.

Introduction
One technique of writing a ghost story is to leave open the possibility of a rational explanation; that is, an ordinary, everyday or scientific reason why something has happened. The element of not knowing for certain whether the supernatural is involved can add to the atmosphere.

- Seeing a ghost is frightening enough, but for the signalman these incidents go beyond mere fear of the unknown. He says:

> "By this time you will fully understand, Sir, ... that what troubles me so dreadfully is the question, What does the spectre mean?"

1. The narrator does not understand this at first; in your own words describe what troubles the signalman so dreadfully.

2. The narrator says:

> His pain of mind was most pitiable to see. It was the mental torture of a conscientious man, oppressed beyond endurance by an unintelligible responsibility involving life.

Rewrite this sentence in your own words.

3. Discuss the significance of the words "For God's sake, clear the way!" spoken by the engine driver and mentioned by the narrator in the final paragraph.

4. Discuss the rational, scientific reason that the narrator gives for the strange appearances. Is there anything is the story, apart from coincidence, that makes this explanation possible? Is there anything that makes it a strong possibility?

© Folens (copiable page)

Other ghost stories

FOCUS

- To examine the techniques of constructing a ghost story by comparing two supernatural tales.

- Read 'A Night at a Cottage' (a ghost story) on pages 58–59. Then compare it with 'The Signalman' by making notes under the headings below.

'The Signalman' by Charles Dickens	**'A Night at a Cottage'** by Richard Hughes
Description of ghost	**Description of ghost**
Details of observer	**Details of observer**
Reason for ghost's appearance	**Reason for ghost's appearance**
Effect on observer	**Effect on observer**

 © Folens (copiable page)

Real or imagined?

FOCUS

- To write an essay discussing whether the incidents in 'The Signalman' are genuinely supernatural.

Essay title

Are the incidents in 'The Signalman' genuinely supernatural, or are they simply the product of the signalman's imagination?

Planning

- To answer this question you need to examine the evidence for both a supernatural explanation and a rational one. Complete the lists below.

Evidence for a supernatural explanation

1. An accident occurred six hours after the signalman gave the alarm.

Evidence that the events were caused by the signalman's imagination

1. The signalman worked alone, in a dark, gloomy place; this could be psychologically disturbing.
2. The signalman claimed that a bell had rung, but the narrator heard nothing.

- Write your essay. Make sure that you:
  - present evidence for both explanations
  - give your conclusion clearly
  - explain why you reached your conclusion.

- This story is fiction, not fact. Discuss whether or not you think Dickens wanted a clear answer to the question. What advantages are there in leaving the ending unclear?

© Folens (copiable page)

Exam passage 1

- Read this extract from 'The Signalman' carefully and then answer all the questions that follow.

In a word, I should have set this man down as one of the safest men to be employed in that capacity, but for the circumstance that while he was speaking to me he twice broke off with a fallen colour, turned his face towards the little bell when it did NOT ring, opened the door of the hut (which was kept shut to exclude the unhealthy damp), and looked out towards the red light near the mouth of the tunnel. On both of those occasions, he came back to the fire with an inexplicable air upon him which I had remarked, without being able to define, when we were so far asunder.

Said I when I rose to leave him, "You almost make me think that I have met with a contented man."

(I am afraid I must acknowledge that I said it to lead him on.)

"I believe I used to be so," he rejoined, in the low voice in which he had first spoken; "but I am troubled, Sir, I am troubled."

He would have recalled the words if he could. He had said them, however, and I took them up quickly.

"With what? What is your trouble?"

"It is very difficult to impart, Sir. It is very, very difficult to speak of. If ever you make me another visit, I will try to tell you."

"But I expressly intend to make you another visit. Say, when shall it be?"

"I go off early in the morning, and I shall be on again at ten tomorrow night, sir."

"I will come at eleven."

He thanked me, and went out at the door with me. "I'll show my white light, Sir" he said, in his peculiar low voice, "till you have found the way up. When you have found it, don't call out! And when you are at the top, don't call out!"

His manner seemed to make the place strike colder to me, but I said no more than "Very well."

These questions are all based on the passage.

1. What actions make the narrator wonder about the reliability of the signalman?
2. What was the narrator's reason for suggesting to the signalman that he was a 'contented man'?
3. Sum up the appearance and actions of the signalman in a sentence of your own.

This question is based on the story as a whole.

4. How does Dickens build up suspense in the story? Consider:
   - the language used
   - the setting
   - the structure of the story.

 © Folens (copiable page)

Home life

FOCUS

- To compare and contrast two novels with similar subject matter.

This extract comes from the opening part of *A Kestrel for a Knave* by Barry Hines. You will be asked to compare this with Chapter 2 of *Great Expectations*, so it would be useful to reread that chapter.

"Do me a favour, love, and run up to t'shop for some fags."

"They'll not be open yet."

"You can go to t'back door. Mr Hardy'll not mind."

"I can't, I'll be late."

"Go on, love, and bring a few things back wi' you; a loaf and some butter, and a few eggs, summat like that."

"Go your sen."

"I've not time. Just tell him to put it in t'book and I'll pay him at t'weekend."

"He says you can't have owt else 'til you've paid up."

"He always says that. I'll give you a tanner if you go."

"I don't want a tanner. I'm off now."

He moved towards the door, but his mother stepped across and blocked his way.

"Billy, get up to that shop and do as you're telled."

He shook his head. His mother stepped forward, but he backed off, keeping the same distance between them. Although she was too far away, she still swiped at him, and although he saw her hand coming and going, well clear of his face, he still flicked his head back instinctively.

"I'm not going."

He moved behind the table.

"Aren't you? We'll see about that."

They faced each other across the table, their fingers spread on the cloth, like two pianists ready to begin.

"We'll see whether you're going or not, you cheeky young bugger."

Billy moved to his right. His mother to her left. He stood out from the corner, so that only the length of one side separated them. His mother grabbed for him. Billy shot across the back of the table and round the other corner, but his mother was back in position, waiting. She lunged forward, Billy skipped back and they faced up again from their original positions.

"I'll bloody murder you when I get hold of you.

"Gi'o'er now, mam, I'll be late for school."

You'll be more than late, unless you do as you're telled."

"He said I'd get t'stick next time."

"That's nowt to what you'll get if I catch you."

Billy ducked down. His mother followed, holding on to the table top to retain balance. They faced each other under the table, then Billy feinted a move forward. His mother dived, at nothing. Billy jumped up and ran round the table while his mother was still full stretch on the floor.

"Billy come back. Do you hear? I said come back!"

He whipped the kitchen door open and ran out into the garden. He was half-way down the path when his mother appeared, panting and jabbing her finger at him.

"Just you wait lad! Just you wait 'til tonight!"

1. Discuss what you learn about the character of Billy and his mother, and their background, from this extract.
2. After your discussion, make a list of the similarities and differences between the description of home life in this extract, and the description of Pip's home life in Chapter 2 of *Great Expectations*.
3. Based on the two extracts, write a brief comparison between Billy's mother and Mrs Joe.

© Folens (copiable page)

Class distinction

FOCUS

- To compare the way Billy and Pip are viewed by people who consider themselves socially superior.

Read these three extracts. The first is from *A Kestrel for a Knave* and the other two are from *Great Expectations*.

"You know what they said when I took you on, don't you?"
He waited, as though expecting Billy to supply the answer.
"They said, you'll have to keep your eyes open now, you know, 'cos they're all alike off that estate. They'll take your breath if you're not careful."
"I've never taken owt o' yours, have I?"
"I've never given you chance, that's why."
"You don't have to. I've stopped getting into trouble now."
Porter opened his mouth, blinked, then pulled his watch out and studied the time.
"Are you going to stand there all day, then?"
He shook the watch and placed it to one ear.
"Next thing I know, everybody? be ringing me up and asking why I can't deliver on time."

"Let me see you play cards with this boy."
"With this boy! Why, he is a common labouring-boy! ..."
"He calls the knaves, Jacks, this boy!" said Estella with disdain, before our first game was out. "And what coarse hands he has. And what thick boots!"

"And when it come to character, warn't it Compeyson as had been to the school, and warn't it his schoolfellows as was in this position and in that, and warn't it him as had been know'd by witnesses in such clubs and societies, and nowt to his disadvantage? And warn't it me as had been tried afore, and as had been know'd up hill and down dale in Bridewells and Lock-Ups? And when it came to speech-making, warn't it Compeyson as could speak to 'em wi' his face dropping every now and then into his white pocket-handkercher – ah! and wi' verses in his speech, too – and warn't it me as could only say, 'Gentleman, this man at my side is a most precious rascal'? And when the verdict come, warn't it Compeyson as was recommended to mercy on account of good character and bad company, and giving up all the information he could agen me, and warn't it me as got never a word but Guilty?"

1. Discuss the attitude of the newsagent, Porter, to Billy and compare it with Estella's attitude to Pip and the court's attitude to Magwitch and Compeyson. Do you think these attitudes are fair or prejudiced?

2. Now you have discussed this, read this second extract from *A Kestrel for a Knave*. It comes immediately before the first extract. Discuss whether this changes your feelings about the newsagent and Billy.

   Billy reached out and lifted two bars of chocolate from a display table at the side of the counter. He dropped them into his bag as Porter turned round.

 © Folens (copiable page)

Punishment and justice

FOCUS

- To compare and contrast the behaviour of adult authority towards children in *A Kestrel for a Knave* and *Great Expectations*.

- Billy has fallen asleep in assembly and has been sent to the headmaster, Mr Gryce. There are three other boys there who have been caught smoking, including MacDowell, the school bully. Another boy sent to Mr Gryce with a message from one of the teachers also waits. The smokers know that they will be searched and make the boy with the message put their cigarettes in his pockets …

"It's fantastic isn't it, that in this day and age, in this super-scientific, all-things-bright-and-splendiferous age, that the only way of running this school efficiently is by the rule of the cane. But why? There should be no need for it now. You lot have got it on a plate.

"I can understand why we had to use it back in the 'twenties and 'thirties. Those were hard times; they bred hard people, and it needed hard measures to deal with them. But those times bred people with qualities totally lacking in you people today. They bred people with respect for a start. We knew where we stood in those days, and even today a man will often stop me in the street and say 'Hello Mr Gryce, remember me?' And we'll pass the time of day and chat, and he'll laugh about the thrashings I gave him.

"But what do I get from you lot? A honk from a greasy youth behind the wheel of some big second-hand car. Or an obscene remark from a gang – after they've passed me.

"They took it then, but not now, not in this day of the common man, when every boy quotes his rights, and shoots off home for his father as soon as I look at him.... No guts ... No backbone ... you've nothing to commend you whatsoever. You're just fodder for the mass media!"

He slashed the stick in front of their chests, making the air swish in its wake, then he turned round and leaned straight-armed on the mantelshelf, shaking his head. The boys winked at each other.

"I don't know. I just don't know."

He turned round slowly. The boys met him with serious expressions, frowning and compressing their lips as though they were trying their hardest to solve his problems.

"So for want of a better solution I continue using the cane, knowing full well that you'll be back time and time again for some more. Knowing that when you smokers leave this room wringing your hands, you'll carry on smoking just the same. Yes, you can smirk. lad. I'll bet your pockets are ladened up at this very moment in readiness for break; aren't they? Aren't they? Well just empty them. Come on, all of you, empty your pockets!"

The three smokers, Billy and MacDowall began to reveal their collected paraphernalia. The messenger watched them in panic, the colour rising in his face like the warming bar of an electric fire. He stepped forward again.

"Please, Sir ..."

"Quiet, lad! And get your pockets emptied!"

1. Discuss Mr Gryce's attitude to the boys at his school. Do you find it reasonable or unreasonable? Why?
2. Mr Gryce admits that the use of corporal punishment is ineffective. Discuss how he justifies its use.
3. Write a short comparison between Mr Gryce and Mr Jaggers. Base your work on the extract above and the impression gained of Mr Jaggers in Chapter 18 of *Great Expectations*.

© Folens (copiable page)

Comparison between Billy and Pip

FOCUS

- To compare the characters of Billy in *A Kestrel for a Knave* and the young Pip in *Great Expectations*.

- Use this sheet to plan a written comparison of Billy and Pip as a child, based on your reading of *A Kestrel for a Knave* and *Great Expectations*.

Home background	Behaviour	Your own thoughts on the characters of the two boys
Pip	Pip	Pip
Billy	Billy	Billy

- In a final paragraph, say which boy you find the most likeable and why.

© Folens (copiable page)

The Gorbals and Barnard's Inn

FOCUS

- To compare descriptions of place from a poem and a novel.

- This poem, 'Glasgow Sonnet' by Edwin Morgan, describes the Gorbals, a once very poor area of Glasgow. The extract following it is from Chapter 21 of *Great Expectations* and describes Barnard's Inn. Read both pieces.

A mean wind wanders through the backcourt trash.
Hackles on puddles rise, old mattresses
puff briefly and subside. Play fortresses
of brick and bric-a-brac spill out some ash.
Four storeys have no windows left to smash,
but in the fifth a chipped sill buttresses
mother and daughter, the last mistresses
of that black block condemned to stand, not crash.
Around them the cracks deepen, the rats crawl.
The kettle whimpers on a crazy hob.
Roses of mould grow from ceiling to wall.
The man lies late since he has lost his job,
smokes on one elbow, letting his coughs fall
thinly into an air too poor to rob.

Edwin Morgan

I now found Barnard to be a disembodied spirit, or a fiction, and his inn the dingiest collection of shabby buildings ever squeezed together in a rank corner as a club for Tom-cats.

We entered this haven through a wicket-gate, and were disgorged by an introductory passage into a melancholy little square that looked to me like a flat burying-ground. I thought it had the most dismal trees in it, and the most dismal sparrows, and the most dismal cats, and the most dismal houses (in number half a dozen or so), that I had ever seen. I thought the windows of the sets of chambers into which these houses were divided, were in every stage of dilapidated blind and curtain, crippled flower-pot, cracked glass, dusty decay, and miserable makeshift; while To Let To Let To Let, glared at me from empty rooms, as if no new wretches ever came there, and the vengeance of the soul of Barnard were being slowly appeased by the gradual suicide of the present occupants and their unholy interment under the gravel. A frouzy mourning of soot and smoke attired this forlorn creation of Barnard, and it had strewn ashes on its head, and was undergoing penance and humiliation as a mere dust-hole. Thus far my sense of sight; while dry rot and wet rot and all the silent rots that rot in neglected roof and cellar – rot of rat and mouse and bug and coaching-stables near at hand besides – addressed themselves faintly to my sense of smell, and moaned, "Try Barnard's Mixture."

1. Discuss the similarities and differences in the style of Edwin Morgan and Charles Dickens in these two extracts. In particular, consider the difference made by Dickens' use of the first person.

2. After your discussion, write a comparison between the two extracts.

© Folens (copiable page)

Comparisons

FOCUS

- To read and compare two ghost stories.

- Read this short story, 'A Night at a Cottage', by Richard Hughes. You will be asked to make a comparison with Charles Dickens' 'The Signalman', so bear that story in mind as you read this one.

On the evening that I am considering I passed by some ten or twenty cosy barns and sheds without finding one to my liking: for Worcestershire lanes are devious and muddy, and it was nearly dark when I found an empty cottage set back from the road in a little bedraggled garden. There had been heavy rain earlier in the day, and the straggling fruit trees still wept over it.

But the roof looked sound, there seemed no reason why it should not be fairly dry inside – as dry, at any rate, as I was likely to find anywhere.

I decided: and with a long look up the road and a long look down the road, I drew an iron bar from the lining of my coat and forced the door, which was only held by a padlock and two staples. Inside, the darkness was damp and heavy: I struck a match, and with its haloed light I saw the black mouth of a passage somewhere ahead of me: and then it spluttered out. So I closed the door carefully, though I had little reason to fear passers-by at such a dismal hour in so remote a lane: and lighting another match, I crept down this passage to a little room at the far end, where the air was a bit clearer, for all that the window was boarded across. Moreover, there was a little rusted stove in this room: and thinking it too dark for any to see the smoke, I ripped up part of the wainscot with my knife, and soon was boiling my tea over a bright, small fire, and drying some of the day's rain out of my steamy clothes. Presently I piled the stove with wood to its top bar, and setting my boots where they would best dry, I stretched my body out to sleep.

I cannot have slept very long, for when I woke the fire was still burning brightly. It is not easy to sleep for long together on the level boards of a floor, for the limbs grow numb, and any movement wakes. I turned over, and was about to go again to sleep when I was startled to hear steps in the passage. As I have said, the window was boarded, and there was no other door from the little room – no cupboard even – in which to hide. It occurred to me rather grimly that there was nothing to do but to sit up and face the music, and that would probably mean being hauled back to Worcester Jail, which I had left two bare days before, and where, for various reasons, I had no anxiety to be seen again.

The stranger did not hurry himself but presently walked slowly down the passage, attracted by the light of the fire: and when he came in he did not seem to notice me where I lay huddled in a corner, but walked straight over to the stove and warmed his hands at it. He was dripping wet; wetter than I should have thought it possible for a man to get, even on such a rainy night: and his clothes were old and worn. The water dripped from him on to the floor: he wore no hat, and the straight hair over his eyes dripped water that sizzled spitefully on the embers.

It occurred to me at once that he was no lawful citizen, but another wanderer like myself; a gentleman of the Road; so I gave him some sort of greeting, and we were presently in conversation. He complained much of the cold and wet, and huddled himself over the fire, his teeth chattering and his face an ill white.

"No," I said, "it is no decent weather for the Road, this. But I wonder this cottage isn't more frequented, for it's a tidy little bit of a cottage."

Outside the pale dead sunflowers and giant weeds stirred in the rain.

Comparisons (continued)

"Time was", he answered, "there wasn't a tighter little cot in the co-anty, nor a purtier garden. A regular little parlour, she was. But now no folk'll live in it and there's very few tramps will stop here either."

There were none of the rags and tins and broken food about that you find in a place where many beggars are used to stay.

"Why's that?" I asked

He gave a very troubled sigh before answering.

"Gho-asts," he said; "gho-asts. Him that lived here. It is a mighty sad tale, and I'll not tell it you: but the upshot of it was that he drowned himself, down to the mill-pond. All slimy, he was, and floating, when they pulled him out of it. There are fo-aks have seen un floating on the pond, and fo-aks have seen un round the corner of the school, waiting for his childer. Seems as if he had forgotten, like, how they were all gone dead, and the why he drowned hisself. But there are some say he walks up and down this cottage, up and down; like when the small-pox had 'em, and they couldn't sleep but if they heard his feet going up and down by their do-ars. Drownded hisself down to the pond, he did: and now he Walks."

The stranger sighed again, and I could hear the water squelch in his boots as he moved himself.

"But it doesn't do for the like of us to get superstitious," I answered. "It wouldn't do for us to get seeing ghosts, or many's the wet night we'd be lying in the roadway."

"No," he said; "no, it wouldn't do at all. I never had belief in Walks myself."

I laughed.

"Nor I that," I said. "I never see ghosts, whoever may."

He looked at me again in his queer melancholy fashion.

"No," he said. "'Spect you don't ever. Some folk do-an't. It's hard enough for poor fellows to have no money to their lodging, apart from gho-asts sceering them."

"It's the coppers, not spooks, make me sleep uneasy," said I. "What with coppers, and meddlesome-minded folk, it isn't easy to get a night's rest nowadays."

The water was still oozing from his clothes all about the floor, and a dank smell went up from him.

"God! man," I cried, "can't you never get dry?"

"Dry?" He made a little coughing laughter. "Dry? I shan't never be dry … 'tisn't the likes of us that ever get dry, be it wet or fine, winter or summer. See that."

He thrust his muddy hands up to the wrist in the fire, glowering over it fiercely and madly. But I caught up my two boots and ran crying out into the night.

- Write a comparison between this story and 'The Signalman'. In your comparison, you should consider:
  - how atmosphere and tension are created
  - the structure of the story
  - the characters of the two narrators and their attitudes to the supernatural.

  In your final paragraph, say which story you prefer, and why.

Exam passage 2

- Read this passage carefully and then answer all the questions that follow.

"What I had to say to Estella, Miss Havisham, I will say before you, presently – in a few moments. It will not surprise you, it will not displease you. I am as unhappy as you can ever have meant me to be."

Miss Havisham continued to look steadily at me. I could see in the action of Estella's fingers as they worked, that she attended to what I said: but she did not look up.

"I have found out who my patron is. It is not a fortunate discovery, and is not likely ever to enrich me in reputation, station, fortune, anything. There are reasons why I must say no more of that. It is not my secret, but another's."

As I was silent for a while, looking at Estella and considering how to go on, Miss Havisham repeated, "It is not your secret, but another's. Well?"

"When you first caused me to be brought here, Miss Havisham; when I belonged to the village over yonder, that I wish I had never left; I suppose I did really come here, as any other chance boy might have come – as a kind of servant, to gratify a want or a whim, and to be paid for it?"

"Ay, Pip," replied Miss Havisham, steadily nodding her head; "you did."

"And that Mr Jaggers –"

"Mr Jaggers", said Miss Havisham, taking me up in a firm tone, "had nothing to do with it, and knew nothing of it. His being my lawyer, and his being the lawyer of your patron, is a coincidence. He holds the same relation towards numbers of people, and it might easily arise. Be that as it may, it did arise, and was not brought about by any one."

Any one might have seen in her haggard face that there was no suppression or evasion so far.

"But when I fell into the mistake I have so long remained in, at least you led me on?" said I.

"Yes," she returned, again nodding steadily, "I let you go on".

"Was that kind?"

"Who am I," cried Miss Havisham, striking her stick upon the floor and flashing into wrath so suddenly that Estella glanced up at her in surprise, "who am I, for God's sake, that I should be kind!"

It was a weak complaint to have made, and I had not meant to make it. I told her so, as she sat brooding after this outburst.

These questions are all based on the passage.

1. Why does Pip say that Miss Havisham will not be surprised or displeased by what he has to say?
2. What clues are there that Miss Havisham is now telling the truth?
3. What impression is given of Miss Havisham in this passage?

This question is based on the book as a whole.

4. Compare and contrast the character of Pip as it is shown here with the way Pip behaved during previous visits to Miss Havisham.

 © Folens (copiable page)

Exam passage 3

- Read this passage carefully and then answer all the questions that follow.

"Joe is a dear good fellow – in fact, I think he is the dearest fellow that ever lived – but he is rather backward in some things. For instance, Biddy, in his learning and his manners."

Although I was looking at Biddy as I spoke, and although she opened her eyes very wide when I had spoken, she did not look at me.

"Oh, his manners! Won't his manners do then?" asked Biddy, plucking a black currant leaf.

"My dear Biddy, they do very well here –"

"Oh! they *do* very well here?" interposed Biddy, looking closely at the leaf in her hand.

"Hear me out – but if I were to remove Joe into a higher sphere, as I shall hope to remove him when I fully come into my property, they would hardly do him justice."

"And don't you think he knows that?" asked Biddy.

It was such a very provoking question (for it had never in the most distant manner occurred to me), that I said, snappishly, "Biddy, what do you mean?"

Biddy having rubbed the leaf to pieces between her hands – and the smell of a black currant bush has ever since recalled to me that evening in the little garden by the side of the lane – said, "Have you never considered that he may be proud?"

"Proud?" I repeated, with disdainful emphasis.

"Oh! there are many kinds of pride," said Biddy, looking full at me and shaking her head; "pride is not all of one kind –"

"Well? What are you stopping for?" said I.

"Not all of one kind," resumed Biddy. "He may be too proud to let any one take him out of a place that he is competent to fill, and fills well and with respect. To tell you the truth, I think he is: though it sounds bold in me to say so, for you must know him far better than I do."

"Now, Biddy," said I, "I am very sorry to see this in you. I did not expect to see this in you. You are envious, Biddy, and grudging. You are dissatisfied on account of my rise in fortune, and you can't help showing it."

"If you have the heart to think so," returned Biddy, "say so. Say so over and over again, if you have the heart to think so."

These questions are all based on the passage.

1. In your own words, explain what Pip wants Biddy to do.
2. Pip and Biddy have different ideas of pride. Explain them in your own words.
3. From your reading of this passage only, what comments would you make on the characters of Pip and Biddy?

This question is based on the novel as a whole.

4. How does Pip's attitude to Joe change throughout the novel? Consider his feelings towards Joe:
   - in early childhood
   - as an apprentice
   - after learning of his 'great expectations'
   - during Joe's visit to London
   - in the later stages of the novel.

© Folens (copiable page)

The life of Pip

FOCUS

- To write an essay on the character of Pip as it changes throughout his life.

Essay title

Compare and contrast the character of Pip as a child, a young man and as a mature adult.

Planning

- In order to answer this question you need to produce a summary of Pip's character at each relevant stage, then find good evidence (including quotations) to back up your point of view. You should have a short introductory paragraph, outlining what you are trying to do, followed by three sections dealing with Pip's life at the three different stages. Conclude your essay by drawing together your ideas, perhaps with a sentence beginning "In this essay I have shown that …"

Pip's character as a child	Evidence

Pip's character as a young man	Evidence

Pip's character as an adult	Evidence

 © Folens (copiable page)

Turning points

FOCUS

- To write an essay drawing on evidence of what you think is the turning point in the book.

Essay title

What, in your opinion, is the key turning point in *Great Expectations*?

Planning

- **Stage 1:** In order to answer this question you will need to make a 'short-list' of key moments, and make notes on each of them. Use a table like the one below.

Turning point	What happened	Impact/importance within the novel
Pip discovers he has great expectations.	Jaggers visits the forge. He tells Pip and Joe the news of Pip's good fortune and asks Joe to release Pip from his indentures.	1. This moment marks the start of a completely new life for Pip. 2. The novel now has a completely new setting. 3. This moment marks a change in Pip's character.

- **Stage 2:** When you have completed your table, adding moments of your own and detailing their importance, share your ideas with a partner and then decide which moment is the most crucial.

- Write your essay. Make sure that you:
  - explain what happens at the 'turning point' you have chosen
  - give plenty of reasons why you consider it to be so important
  - refer to several other moments or events, saying why you consider them less important.

Revenge

FOCUS

- To write an essay based on the theme of revenge in *Great Expectations*.

Essay title

How important is the theme of revenge in *Great Expectations*?

Planning

- **Stage 1:** To answer this, you will need to consider:
  - how often revenge appears in the novel
  - what it contributes to the novel as a whole.

Examples of revenge

Add to this list. Examples of revenge are:
- the way Miss Havisham treats Estella and Pip
- Magwitch's determination to get even with Compeyson.

- **Stage 2:** Discuss these points with a partner and answer the questions. Can you think of any other points?
  - Revenge motivates many of the characters in the novel and is central to our understanding of them. *Which characters?*
  - Readers like to see the guilty punished. *Do you agree? Is this relevant?*
  - The theme provides the main story-lines for the novel. *Which story-lines?*
  - Revenge is the cause of the most exciting action in the novels. *Find any examples; do you agree?*
  - The theme involves the reader in the lives of the characters by getting him or her to take sides. *Do you agree?*

- Now write your essay. Assuming that you think revenge is an important theme (and you probably will!), you will need to include:
  - an introductory paragraph stating your view and how you intend to justify it
  - a section showing how frequently it occurs in the novel and how central it is to the action
  - a section showing what the theme contributes to the novel in other ways
  - a final paragraph summing up the importance of the theme, perhaps compared with another theme you have looked at, such as blighted childhood.

 © Folens (copiable page)